Creative Minds

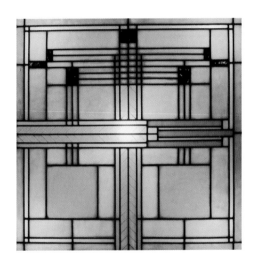

Patricia J. Murphy

TM
sundance
A Haights Cross Communications ® Company

Published by
Sundance Publishing
P.O. Box 740
One Beeman Road
Northborough, MA 01532–0740
800-343-8204
www.sundancepub.com

Creative Minds
ISBN 0-7608-9637-2

Illustrations by Brian Biggs

Photo and Art Credits
Cover ©Sam Barcroft, Barcroft Media Ltd.; p. 1 ©Thomas A. Heinz/CORBIS; p. 6 Erich Lessing/
Art Resource, NY; p. 7 (top) ©CORBIS, (bottom) Digital Image ©The Museum of Modern
Art/Licensed by SCALA/Art Resource, NY, ©2005 The Georgia O'Keeffe Foundation/Artists Rights
Society (ARS), New York; p. 8 Herscovici/Art Resource, NY, ©2005 C. Herscovici, Brussels/Artists
Rights Society (ARS), New York; p. 9 (left) Photothèque R. Magritte-ADAGP/Art Resource, NY,
©2005 C. Herscovici, Brussels/Artists Rights Society (ARS), New York, (right) M.C. Escher's "Print
Gallery" ©2005 The M.C. Escher Company-Holland. All rights reserved. www.msescher.com;
p. 10 (top) ©Philippe Halsman Estate/Courtesy Howard Greenberg Gallery, NYC, (bottom)
©Film Rental/Courtesy Museum Masters International NY, ©2005 Salvador Dali, Gala-Salvador
Dali Foundation/Artists Rights Society (ARS), New York; p. 11 (top) Digital Image ©The Museum
of Modern Art/Licensed by SCALA/Art Resource, NY, ©2005 Salvador Dali, Gala-Salvador Dali
Foundation/Artists Rights Society (ARS), New York, (bottom) ©1993 Donato Giancola; p. 14
(top) ©Sam Barcroft, Barcroft Media Ltd., (left) ©Leo Sewell; pp. 14–15 ©Leo Sewell; p. 16
Tony Vaccaro/Getty Images; pp. 16–17 Giraudon/Art Resource, NY, ©2005 Estate of Lousie
Nevelson/Artists Rights Society (ARS), New York; p. 17 Digital Image ©The Museum of
Modern Art/Licensed by SCALA/Art Resource, NY, ©2005 Artists Rights Society (ARS), New
York/ProLitteris, Zürich; p. 18 (left) ©Chuck Pefley/Alamy, (bottom) ©Dennis Macdonald/Index
Stock Imagery, Inc.; p. 19 (left) ASAP Ltd./Index Stock Imagery, Inc., (bottom) ©Joern
Sackermann/Alamy; p. 20, 21 ©Craig Nutt; p. 24 (left) ©Thomas A. Heinz/CORBIS, (right)
©Richard A. Cooke/CORBIS; p. 25 (full page) ©Angelo Hornak/CORBIS, (inset) ©Roger Wood/
CORBIS; p. 26 (top) ©David Butow/CORBIS SABA, (left) ©Marvin Koner/CORBIS; p. 27 (top)
©Richard Sobol/ZUMA/Corbis, (bottom) ©Nik Wheeler/CORBIS; p. 28 (full page) ©Wolfgang
Kaehler/CORBIS, (inset) John James Wood/Index Stock Imagery, Inc.; p. 29 (top) ©1991 Roger
Ressmeyer; Fish & Furniture ©Frank Gehry & New City Editions/CORBIS, (bottom) ©Yann
Arthus-Bertrand/CORBIS

Printed in Canada

Table of Contents

Seeing Things Differently

Imagine living in a world of gigantic flowers, melting watches, and faces made of fruits and vegetables. This world exists— inside the artist's mind.

We all live in the same world and look at the same things. But artists see these things very differently. We know this by the paintings they paint. An Italian artist, for example, pictured clumps of vegetables and other things in place of human features. At first glance they look human, but when you take a closer look, you'll see peas instead of eyelids and a pear for a nose!

An artist's paintings can even make us look at things differently. One American artist painted close-ups of huge flowers. Looking at them makes you think about their beauty. Other painters show us things that are scary or funny to them. Let's take a closer look.

Giuseppe Arcimboldo

Lots of artists have painted bowls of fruit and vases of flowers. But some artists paint these things in very different ways!

The *Vegetable Gardener* is a bowl of vegetables—or is it? Turn it upside down, and now it's a man.

Fruit Face

More than 500 years ago, Giuseppe Arcimboldo painted portraits. But his were not like other **portraits**. The faces didn't have realistic features like eyes or noses. Instead, he painted collections of flowers and fruits to look like eyes and noses.

And with a blink of an eye, his paintings change. Look at the portrait of *Vertumnus.* Do you see an emperor's head or lots of separate pieces of fruit?

Do you think green is my color?

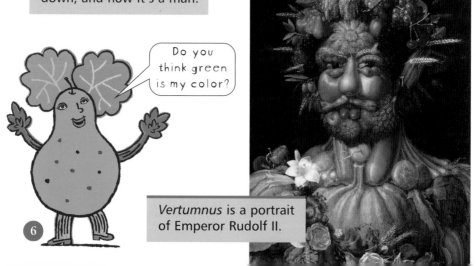

Vertumnus is a portrait of Emperor Rudolf II.

Georgia O'Keeffe

A famous photographer—who later married her—saw Georgia O'Keeffe's paintings and exclaimed, "At last a woman on paper!"

Take Time to Look

Georgia O'Keeffe is one of America's most successful, important artists. O'Keeffe went to art school and painted what her teachers wanted. But in her late 20s, she began to paint what she really felt.

Georgia O'Keeffe used colors and shapes like a language to communicate ideas.

O'Keeffe would paint bold colors and shapes onto a huge **canvas**. She often painted enlarged parts of objects, instead of the whole object. When painting her now-famous flowers, she made them huge so that people would have to take the time to look at them. And they did.

O'Keeffe painted big flowers. She said, ". . . I will make even New Yorkers take time to see what I see of flowers."

An Orchid

7

Rene Magritte

Everyday things can become
a bit mysterious if you use them
in unusual ways.

Magically Real

Many of Rene Magritte's paintings
make you do a double take. You
have to come back and look again.
He fills his canvases with surprises
by painting realistic, everyday
things in very unexpected ways.

Simple objects, like shoes,
are painted in a mysterious
way in *Le Modele Rouge*.

La Clairvoyance

Here Margritte shows that the creative
mind can see one thing and paint another.

Magritte's painting style has been labeled "magical realism." Hidden surprises and fantasy-like images look both magical and real. But Magritte didn't want people to try figuring out what his paintings mean. He felt people wouldn't see the poetry and mystery of his images if they kept trying to explain them.

Talking about his painting, Magritte said, "What does it mean? It does not mean anything because mystery means nothing either; it is unknowable."

Le Therapeute

Is It Math or Is It Art?

M.C. Escher was an artist, but some of the people who most admired his works were mathematicians. Escher read about and explored mathematical ideas. Many of his drawings and later works explore the space on the page. In the space on one print, *Print Gallery,* he made the young man appear inside the gallery and outside of it at the same time!

Magritte often painted realistic objects in unrealistic settings.

Salvador Dali

You would not use the word "realistic" to describe the paintings of Salvador Dali!

Is It a Dream?

Have you ever gazed at a cloud for a long time and found many different shapes within the one cloud? This is the same method Dali used to picture images in his mind for his paintings. He called these fantasy, dreamlike paintings "hand painted dream photographs."

Salvador Dali did not always want to be an artist. "At the age of six years, I wanted to be a chef. At the age of seven I wanted to be Napoleon."

When you peek into the **surreal**, frozen scenes in the paintings of Salvador Dali, things can seem very weird. Dali found a way to see the world around him in new and unique ways. He would take ordinary objects and eerily transform them by bending, twisting, or melting them on the canvas. At the time of his death in 1989, he was considered one of the most influential people in modern art.

Dali painted the face of a movie star of long ago as part of a room. This painting is called *Face of Mae West*.

The Persistence of Memory, by Dali

DONATO GIANCOLA

Giancola creates fantasy in his out-of-this-world science fiction art. He makes worlds full of imagination and magic. Where does he get his inspiration? Simply by watching what goes on in the real world!

Donato Giancola has used real models and objects for his fantasy paintings. In the painting for the game "Stratego," he used family members and himself as models for the game pieces!

Construct of Time

11

Changing Everyday Objects

Dumpster diving is a great way for some artists to find all sorts of treasure. Other artists are inspired by ordinary objects— even food!

Junkyards, dumpsters, and lumberyards might not be the kind of places where you would think to look for art treasures. But some sculptors do just that. They make sculptures out of wood scraps, old magic markers, dented spoons, and buttons.

Other sculptors can make you think of everyday objects in a different way. Two artists created a bridge out of an oversized metal spoon. Many people never thought of a spoon as a bridge before—but now they do! Have you ever thought about the shape of a celery stalk or carrot? Well, one artist did. He used wooden carrots for furniture legs! So, to an artist, someone else's trash can be a treasure—and everyday objects can provide great ideas for some far-out art!

Leo Sewell

Leo Sewell is like a deep-sea diver, but he doesn't dive into the sea. He dives into dumps and recycling bins to look for objects to use in his sculptures!

Leo Sewell

Art from the Junk Pile

At the age of 10, Sewell began digging in naval dumps in Annapolis, Maryland. He found all sorts of gadgets and gizmos to take apart and put together. "At the time, I really didn't think it was art," says Sewell, "just fun."

Today, it's still fun for Sewell and for everyone who sees his one-of-a-kind animal sculptures.

Scotty

Stegosaurus Maquette

14

They are made from hundreds of different, often colorful objects that Sewell has found. Each sculpture begins as a basic shape made of found objects. Then Sewell attaches more objects to it with nails, bolts, and screws. He says that the worst thing the eye can see is plainness. So there is nothing plain about his work!

Thousands of Animals

So far, Sewell has created over 3,000 animal sculptures. His *Teddy Bear* includes 15 teddy bear objects. His *Stegosaurus* has a baby stegosaurus! And, his *Coyote* is made of objects donated by kids to the Phoenix Children's Hospital.

WHAT'S IN THAT TEDDY BEAR?

"Chance is a great creative force!" says Sewell. His *Teddy Bear* sculpture, which is 16 inches high and 13 inches wide, is made of hundreds of objects he found by chance. They include a police badge, a corn holder, bracelets, pencils, hair barrettes, and 440 nuts, bolts, and/or screws.

Louise Nevelson

Who could imagine becoming a successful sculptor making walls out of boxes? Louise Nevelson did just that!

Walls of Rubbish

Like Leo Sewell, Louise Nevelson used objects that had been thrown away to create her best-known sculptures. She used things like wood scraps, metal, broken glass, mirrors, and electric lights. First, she arranged them into shallow boxes. Next, she painted them black, white, or gold. Then, she stacked her boxes side by side and on top of each other to create large **abstract** walls. Changes in the light and shadows on Nevelson's walls create mysterious, dreamlike effects.

Always an Artist

Even as a child making sculptures with wood from her father's lumberyard, Nevelson knew art would be her life. And at the age of 89, Nevelson still gathered objects and created her sculptures.

"I never feel age," said Nevelson. "If you have creative work, you don't have age or time."

Nevelson didn't have an art show of just her own work until she was about 40 years old. When she was 60, sales from her art finally helped pay her bills.

MERET OPPENHEIM

If Meret Oppenheim had thrown a tea party, not many people would have come. That's because her most famous sculpture was a teacup, saucer, and spoon covered with fur! While the tea set wasn't for sipping, it was for viewing. The wildly popular "party ware" became the most talked about and copied of her sculptures.

Oppenheim's art certainly opened people's eyes and minds to a new way of using everyday objects as art.

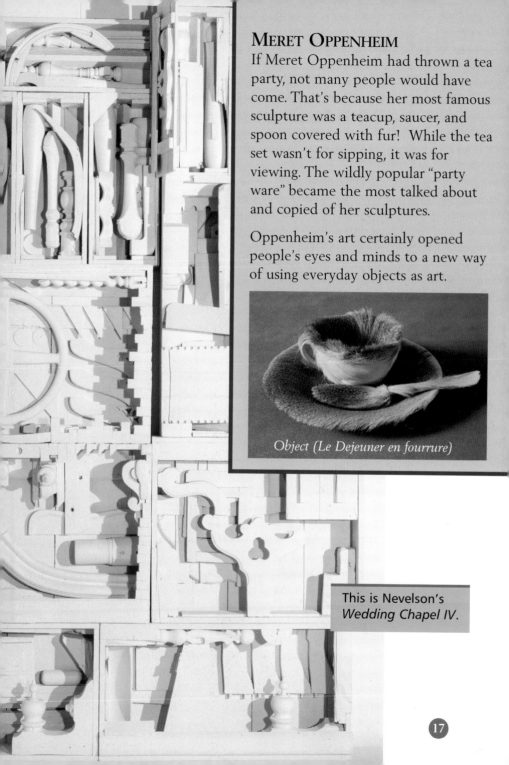

Object (Le Dejeuner en fourrure)

This is Nevelson's *Wedding Chapel IV*.

Supersized Sculptures

Some sculptors choose to enlarge everyday objects. Coming across these pieces of art usually makes people smile—after they get over their surprise!

Claes Oldenburg and Coosje van Bruggen

By playing around with the size, shape, and surface of everyday things, sculptors Oldenburg and van Bruggen change them—and give them new life. Since 1976, the husband-and-wife-team has created over 40 large-scale sculptures that change cities and landscapes around the world. Oldenburg and van Bruggen help people see art in everyday things.

Shuttlecocks

Spoonbridge and Cherry

Their *Spoonbridge and Cherry* sculpture in Minneapolis, Minnesota, is a 51-foot-long, stainless steel and aluminum spoon bridge with a 1,200-pound cherry fountain. In Germany, their sculptures include a giant pickax and an oversized faucet with a twisted garden hose. In the Netherlands, one of their huge gardening trowels is embedded in the earth. Many passersby love their work. Others aren't so sure what to think, but they usually stop and look.

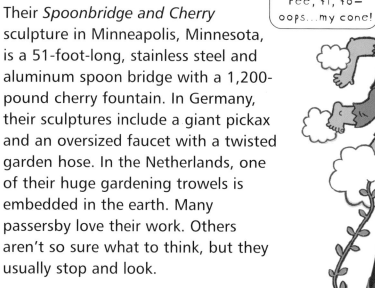

Apple Core

This *Dropped Cone* sculpture was made in California then shipped to Germany to be placed on this building.

Craig Nutt

At home in his vegetable garden or in the produce section at the grocery store, Craig Nutt celebrates the magic of . . . vegetables. Nutt can't get enough of them—whether he's growing them, eating them, or making wooden sculptures of them. "Only nature could think up such brilliant colors and shapes!" explains Nutt.

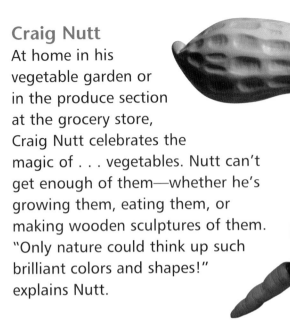

Nutt says, "Most of my work is rooted in vegetables."

Ground Launch Goober

Asparagus, peas, and carrots are included in this Craig Nutt bench.

Burning

Corncorde

To share the wonders of corn, Nutt created the flying *Corncorde*. This 10-foot ear of corn flies high above Gate E16 at Hartsfield-Jackson Atlanta International Airport. Nearby, Nutt's 6-foot *Imperator* carrot with a butterbean clock on top of it helps to keep travelers on time.

Want some celery stalk chairs or a tomato table? Nutt has made them. No vegetable or idea is too nutty for him. "Sometimes, the best ideas are those others might think are stupid . . . ," says Nutt.

Imperator

Airport food is looking better these days!

21

Building Eye-Popping Places

Imagine living in a house that is perched over a splashing waterfall! Or going to school in a building that looks like it might fall over!

Architects plan how buildings will look. They play with space like kids play with building blocks. Kids look at their blocks and decide which block will fit next. Architects look at a space and decide what kind of building will fit best. They think about a building's size and shape and what kind of materials to use. Believe it or not, some buildings even look like they are moving—just because of materials the architect used!

Let's take a look at two famous architects—and the buildings designed by their creative minds.

Frank Lloyd Wright

Who knew that playing with strips of colored paper and wooden blocks could lead to the life of an architect?

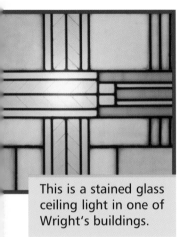

This is a stained glass ceiling light in one of Wright's buildings.

The Wright Stuff

The mother of Frank Lloyd Wright might have known just that! As an adult, the shapes and forms he played with as a child became houses and buildings. Some of these are America's most famous structures.

Wright's **style** of architecture was different from that of other architects. His flatter houses became part of the landscape around them. But he didn't stop with houses— he added his style to hotels, temples, and even museums.

A Snail in the City

Sitting across from Central Park, the Guggenheim Museum designed by Wright looks like a giant snail's shell. Outside, Wright used concrete to create a **spiral** that stands out against the city street. Inside, ramps whirl around a huge open space. Continuous spaces flow into one another to display the works of art.

Fallingwater, one of Wright's designs, is in Pennsylvania.

Wright wanted the Guggenheim building and the art inside to work together like ". . . an uninterrupted, beautiful symphony . . ."

His building and the space inside are completely different from any other museum—just like the abstract and **contemporary** artwork inside. Today, the Guggenheim is considered one of the world's great works of architecture.

Wright made it all work together—the building, the interior space, and the environment.

Frank Lloyd Wright lived to complete the designs for the museum, but he died only six months before the Guggenheim was finished.

FRANK LLOYD WRONG?

Nobody's perfect. No home is perfect either—not even the homes Frank Lloyd designed. Sometimes things sagged. Other times things leaked. In fact, an owner of one of Wright's homes called him to complain that water was leaking onto his dining room table. Wright replied, "Move your chair!" He believed the problem was in the way the building was constructed, NOT in his design.

Frank Gehry

Some call him the other Frank who built the other Guggenheim.

A Place of His Own

Frank Gehry has been called the other Frank. Like Wright, his first name is Frank, and he is an architect who built another unique Guggenheim Museum. Also like Wright, he experimented with materials. He wrapped his home in **corrugated** metal and chain link. He stripped away plaster walls inside to expose the wooden frame. People started to pay attention, and now Frank Gehry has earned his own place in today's world of architecture.

This is Frank Gehry's Stata Center at MIT as it was being built in 2004.

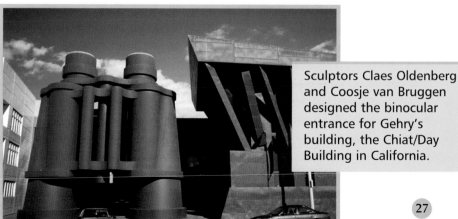

Sculptors Claes Oldenberg and Coosje van Bruggen designed the binocular entrance for Gehry's building, the Chiat/Day Building in California.

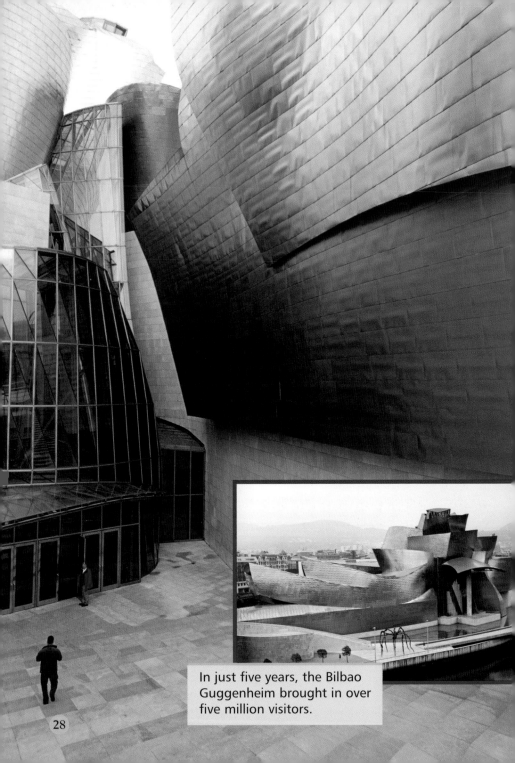

In just five years, the Bilbao Guggenheim brought in over five million visitors.

A Masterpiece in Motion

In the 1990s, Frank Gehry began experimenting with the computer. He would scan in his models and designs. Then he would **manipulate** curves, shapes, and space. He used this technology to create an engineering wonder— the Guggenheim Museum in Bilbao, Spain. Gehry used **titanium** steel and swooping curves that seem to capture the movement of the Bilbao River alongside the site. Some visitors say the building itself appears to move at certain times of the day.

Frank Gehry is also a well-known artist. He uses shapes from nature in his furniture, lamps, and sculptures.

Many people say Gehry's Guggenheim Museum may have changed architecture forever. Today, millions of people come to see it. Prior to this, Bilbao wasn't even a popular city! So Frank Gehry has shown people how powerful and important architecture can be to a city.

Creative minds know no limits!

Another view of the Bilbao Guggenheim

Fact File

Salvador Dali created "dream" scenes for the movie, *Spellbound*. The director, Alfred Hitchcock, wanted "real" looking dreams.

Leo Sewell doesn't get paid in money when he speaks at schools—he gets paid in junk. He charges eight bushels of junk per hour.

Thanks for the junk.

Georgia O'Keeffe had to paint one of her paintings on the side of a two-car garage because the canvas was too big to fit in her studio.

Frank Lloyd Wright's son, Lincoln, invented the "Lincoln logs." Building blocks must have run in their family!

Glossary

abstract a style of art that does not show real objects but uses lines, shapes, and colors

contemporary current or new

canvas a strong, heavy cloth sometimes used for oil paintings

corrugated ridged or wrinkled

manipulate to change by artful means to suit a purpose

portraits artworks that portray a person

spiral a curving, twisting shape or object

style a particular way by which something is done or created

surreal dreamlike or not realistic

titanium silvery-gray metallic material

canvas

Index